REFLECTIONS
FOR
ADVENT

29 November – 24 December 2021

STEPHEN COTTRELL
GULI FRANCIS-DEHQANI

with an introduction to Advent
by LIBBY LANE

At the heart
of Christmas

Church House Publishing
Church House
Great Smith Street
London SW1P 3AZ

ISBN 978 0 7151 2400 0

Published 2021 by Church House Publishing
Copyright © The Archbishops' Council 2021

The opinions expressed in this book are those of the
authors and do not necessarily reflect the official policy of
the General Synod or The Archbishops' Council of the
Church of England.

Liturgical editor: Peter Moger
Series editor: Hugh Hillyard-Parker
Designed and typeset by Hugh Hillyard-Parker
Copy edited by Ros Connelly
Printed by CPI Bookmarque, Croydon, Surrey

What do you think of *Reflections for Daily Prayer*?

We'd love to hear from you – simply email us at

publishing@churchofengland.org

or write to us at

Church House Publishing, Church House,
Great Smith Street, London SW1P 3AZ.

Visit **www.dailyprayer.org.uk** for more
information on the *Reflections* series, ordering
and subscriptions.

Contents

About *Reflections for Advent*

Based on the *Common Worship Lectionary* readings for Morning Prayer, these daily reflections are designed to refresh and inspire times of personal prayer. The aim is to provide rich, contemporary and engaging insights into Scripture.

Each page lists the Lectionary readings for the day, with the main psalms for that day highlighted in **bold**. The collect of the day – either the *Common Worship* collect or the shorter additional collect – is also included.

For those using this book in conjunction with a service of Morning Prayer, the following conventions apply: a psalm printed in parentheses is omitted if it has been used as the opening canticle at that office; a psalm marked with an asterisk may be shortened if desired.

A short reflection is provided on either the Old or New Testament reading. Popular writers, experienced ministers, biblical scholars and theologians have contributed to this series, bringing their own emphases, enthusiasms and approaches to biblical interpretation.

Regular users of Morning Prayer and *Time to Pray* (from *Common Worship: Daily Prayer*) and anyone who follows the Lectionary for their regular Bible reading will benefit from the rich variety of traditions represented in these stimulating and accessible pieces.

This volume also includes both a simple form of *Common Worship* Morning Prayer (see pp. 34–5) and a short form of Night Prayer – also known as Compline – (see pp. 38–41), particularly for the benefit of those readers who are new to the habit of the Daily Office or for any reader while travelling.

About the authors

Stephen Cottrell is the Archbishop of York. He was formerly Bishop of Chelmsford and is a well-known writer and speaker on evangelism, spirituality and catechesis. He is one of the team that produced *Pilgrim*, the popular course for the Christian Journey.

Guli Francis-Dehqani is the Bishop of Chelmsford. She was born in Iran but moved to England following the events of the 1979 Islamic Revolution. Having studied music as an undergraduate, she worked at the BBC for a few years before training for ordination and completing a PhD. She was ordained in 1998 and served as Bishop of Loughborough from 2017 to 2021. She is also the Church of England's first Bishop for Housing.

Libby Lane is the Bishop of Derby. In 2015 she was consecrated as Bishop of Stockport, the Church of England's first woman bishop. She chaired the Diocese of Chester Board of Education and the Foxhill Retreat House. She is Chair of Cranmer Hall Theological College Committee and Vice Chair of The Children's Society.

Rachel Treweek is the Bishop of Gloucester and the first female diocesan bishop in England. She served in two parishes in London and was Archdeacon of Northolt and later Hackney. Prior to ordination she was a speech and language therapist and is a trained practitioner in conflict transformation.

Advent: a season of desire and danger

We try to make Advent visible in our household: we garland the fireplaces and stairs but decorate the foliage gently in purple; each Sunday we light a candle on an Advent wreath; we put up the traditional pine or spruce, but until Christmas Eve it is a Jesse Tree, softly lit, hung daily with simple olive wood images depicting salvation history through the stories of God's people in the Bible. These are outward reminders to us that the season of Advent is not simply a countdown to turkey and tinsel.

It's not that I think we just ought to replace one kind of outward display with another, more pious one. And I'm not a grinch. I enjoy the hospitality of the run-up to Christmas – I spend happy hours preparing stuffings and sauces to accompany our roast dinner. I admire the ways people find time and resource to focus on family and friends – I'm not very good at present-finding, but my (now grown-up) children have the knack of identifying often small, inexpensive or home-made gifts that are just right and show an attentiveness that is not only turned on for Christmas. These things can also be outward reminders of important and precious things – of love and hope and desire.

But the season of Advent demands inner work to find real truth under these outward displays. Although I say the Daily Prayers of the Church of England regularly, and find that rhythm and discipline valuable for my own walk with God and vital in maintaining my sense of belonging to the wider Church, Advent is one of seasons of the year when I find my desire to be drawn closer to God grows. The reflections in this book are a resource for the inner work of Advent.

Advent should be full of desire: 'come, Lord Jesus … even so, come'.

That desire is, I think, wonderfully subversive. This season, if taken seriously, strips away all self-reliance and undercuts our hubris. If we allow it to, the eternal hopeful themes of the season can reveal the lack of substance in the relentless consumerism of the public face of the approach to Christmas.

Amid all the noise and activity of December, Advent is the thundering silence of God, putting all our striving to shame, reminding us that we cannot save ourselves or, in the end, hide from God.

Advent is an arrival not an avoidance, a facing up to the truth, a confronting of 'big' things – death, judgement, heaven and hell. Advent requires that we look backwards, and forwards, and inwards. Advent is an asking to see God face to face.

It is, therefore, a momentous, seismic season. A season of daring that passes largely unnoticed now. Entering into this season risks everything. It offers a perspective that reverses and upturns the views we too easily accept. It takes courage to journey through Advent. There is no hiding, no wrapping the truth up with ribbon and baubles. Advent cannot be domesticated or infantilized.

Advent is full of contradiction: knowing all has been fulfilled, we nonetheless yearn with anticipation. And, I think, the extraordinary, outrageous mercy of Advent is the discovery that, as we yearn for Christ's coming – in both humility and glory – we discover that God has always risked trusting the outworking of salvation to the stuff of creation and to human flesh.

Advent challenges us to trust ourselves as much as God trusts us.

In his poem 'Annunciation' from *Walking backwards to Christmas*, Bishop Stephen Cottrell wrote about the danger of a lack of trust. I leave you with the words of that poem and pray that the reflections in this book encourage you, this season of Advent, to dare to trust:

> *There is only one thing that prevents*
> *The gentle movement, heaven into earth:*
> *Not the fear that godly greeting brings,*
> *Nor cold presumption (God could never speak),*
> *Nor empty tomb, nor barren heart,*
> *Nor eyes searching, voices how long blaze,*
> *Nor the silence where there should be praise,*
> *Nor the bitter taste of human failing:*
> *But the lack of trust that what was promised*
> *Might in human flesh be born, achieved,*
> *How happy she who for us all believed,*
> *Strength of God in human weakness blending,*
> *Tenderly the humble servant lifted,*
> *From foetal cry the fatal mending.*

+Libby Lane

Building daily prayer into daily life

In our morning routines, there are many tasks we do without giving much thought to them, and others that we do with careful attention. Daily prayer and Bible reading is a strange mixture of these. These are disciplines (and gifts) that we as Christians should have in our daily pattern, but they are not tasks to be ticked off. Rather they are a key component of our developing relationship with God. In them is *life* – for the fruits of this time are to be lived out by us – and to be most fruitful, the task requires both purpose and letting go.

In saying a daily office of prayer, we make the deliberate decision to say 'yes' to spending time with God – the God who is always with us. In prayer and attentive reading of the Scriptures, there is both a conscious entering into God's presence and a 'letting go' of all we strive to control: both are our acknowledgement that it is God who is God.

> *... come into his presence with singing ...*
>
> *Know that the Lord is God.*
> *It is he that has made us, and we are his;*
> *we are his people, and the sheep of his pasture.*
>
> *Enter his gates with thanksgiving...*
>
> *(Psalm 100, a traditional Canticle at Morning Prayer)*

If we want a relationship with someone to deepen and grow, we need to spend time with that person. It can be no surprise that the same is true between us and God.

In our daily routines, I suspect that most of us intentionally look in the mirror; occasionally we might see beyond the surface of our external reflection and catch a glimpse of who we truly are. For me, a regular pattern of daily prayer and Bible reading is like a hard look in a clean mirror: it gives a clear reflection of myself, my life and the world in which I live. But it is more than that, for in it I can also see the reflection of God who is most clearly revealed in Jesus Christ and present with us now in the Holy Spirit.

This commitment to daily prayer is about our relationship with the God who is love. St Paul, in his great passage about love, speaks of now seeing 'in a mirror, dimly' but one day seeing face to face: 'Now I know only in part; then I will know fully, even as I have been fully known' (1 Corinthians 13.12). Our daily prayer is part of that seeing in a mirror dimly, and it is also part of our deep yearning for an ever-clearer vision of our God. As we read Scripture, the past and the future converge in the present moment. We hear words from long ago – some of which can appear strange and confusing – and yet, the Holy Spirit is living and active in the present. In this place of relationship and revelation, we open ourselves to the possibility of being changed, of being reshaped in a way that is good for us and all creation.

It is important that the words of prayer and Scripture should penetrate deep within rather than be a mere veneer. A quiet location is therefore a helpful starting point. For some, domestic circumstances or daily schedule make that difficult, but it is never impossible to become more fully present to God. The depths of our being can still be accessed no matter the world's clamour and activity. An awareness of this is all part of our journey from a false sense of control to a place of letting go, to a place where there is an opportunity for transformation.

Sometimes in our attention to Scripture, there will be connection with places of joy or pain; we might be encouraged or provoked or both. As we look and see and encounter God more deeply, there will be thanksgiving and repentance; the cries of our heart will surface as we acknowledge our needs and desires for ourselves and the world. The liturgy of Morning Prayer gives this voice and space.

I find it helpful to begin Morning Prayer by lighting a candle. This marks my sense of purpose and my acknowledgement of Christ's presence with me. It is also a silent prayer for illumination as I prepare to be attentive to what I see in the mirror, both of myself and of God. Amid the revelation of Scripture and the cries of my heart, the constancy of the tiny flame bears witness to the hope and light of Christ in all that is and will be.

When the candle is extinguished, I try to be still as I watch the smoke disappear. For me, it is symbolic of my prayers merging with the day. I know that my prayer and the reading of Scripture are not the smoke and mirrors of delusion. Rather, they are about encounter and discovery as I seek to venture into the day to love and serve the Lord as a disciple of Jesus Christ.

+ *Rachel Treweek*

Lectio Divina – a way of reading the Bible

Lectio Divina is a contemplative way of reading the Bible. It dates back to the early centuries of the Christian Church and was established as a monastic practice by Benedict in the sixth century. It is a way of praying the Scriptures that leads us deeper into God's word. We slow down. We read a short passage more than once. We chew it over slowly and carefully. We savour it. Scripture begins to speak to us in a new way. It speaks to us personally, and aids that union we have with God through Christ, who is himself the Living Word.

Make sure you are sitting comfortably. Breathe slowly and deeply. Ask God to speak to you through the passage that you are about to read.

This way of praying starts with our silence. We often make the mistake of thinking prayer is about what we say to God. It is actually the other way round. God wants to speak to us. He will do this through the Scriptures. So don't worry about what to say. Don't worry if nothing jumps out at you at first. God is patient. He will wait for the opportunity to get in. He will give you a word and lead you to understand its meaning for you today.

First reading: Listen

As you read the passage listen for a word or phrase that attracts you. Allow it to arise from the passage as if it is God's word for you today. Sit in silence repeating the word or phrase in your head.

Then say the word or phrase aloud.

Second reading: Ponder

As you read the passage again, ask how this word or phrase speaks to your life and why it has connected with you. Ponder it carefully. Don't worry if you get distracted – it may be part of your response to offer to God. Sit in silence and then frame a single sentence that begins to say aloud what this word or phrase says to you.

Third reading: Pray

As you read the passage for the last time, ask what Christ is calling from you. What is it that you need to do or consider or relinquish or take on as a result of what God is saying to you in this word or phrase? In the silence that follows the reading, pray for the grace of the Spirit to plant this word in your heart.

If you are in a group, talk for a few minutes and pray with each other.

If you are on your own, speak your prayer to God either aloud or in the silence of your heart.

If there is time, you may even want to read the passage a fourth time, and then end with the same silence before God with which you began.

+Stephen Cottrell

Monday 29 November

Matthew 12.1-21

'Here is my servant, whom I have chosen' (v.18)

Today's reading tells two stories of Jesus stretching and challenging the Jewish understanding of the Sabbath. He explains to them that the Sabbath is a gift from God, not just a narrow rule about abstention from work, and good and necessary work can be done.

However, the climax of the passage lies beyond the stories. Matthew quotes the prophet Isaiah, saying: 'Here is my servant, whom I have chosen, my beloved, with whom my soul is well pleased.' These words echo the words that Jesus heard at his baptism. His ministry begins with, and is fuelled by, the affirmation of God's love for Jesus and God's pleasure in him. This affirmation is available to all of us.

The Advent season also has these stories and proclamations at their heart. We are getting ready not just to celebrate the birth of Jesus, but to prepare for that day when we see God face to face. That is the endless Sabbath of God's kingdom, where we enjoy God's company and only do work that is good.

The religious establishment is confounded by Jesus, but because he reinterprets and fulfils the teaching of Judaism in such a compelling and life-giving way, the crowds follow him. But Isaiah takes us one step further. He says that what we see and experience in Jesus is for the whole world. The season of Advent is about the coming of Christ as ruler and judge of everything.

COLLECT

Almighty God,
give us grace to cast away the works of darkness
and to put on the armour of light,
now in the time of this mortal life,
in which your Son Jesus Christ came to us in great humility;
that on the last day,
when he shall come again in his glorious majesty
    to judge the living and the dead,
we may rise to the life immortal;
through him who is alive and reigns with you,
in the unity of the Holy Spirit,
one God, now and for ever.

10 | *Reflection by* **Stephen Cottrell**

Psalms 47, 147.1-12
Ezekiel 47.1-12
or Ecclesiasticus 14.20-end
John 12.20-32

Tuesday 30 November
Andrew the Apostle

John 12.20-32

'... where I am, there will my servant be also' (v.26)

In today's' reading on the Feast Day of St Andrew, we build on some of the words and ideas we looked at yesterday. Quoting Isaiah, 'Here is my servant, whom I have chosen,' Matthew was making an editorial point about Jesus. Today, Jesus says of those who follow him: '... where I am, there will my servant be also'.

Judgement is one of the great Advent themes. There will be a day of reckoning, that day when we see God face to face. Things that are in darkness will be brought to light. We will say more about this as we travel through the Advent season. But Jesus tells us that the main criterion by which we will be judged is whether we served others. And it's no good saying that we didn't see Jesus hungry or naked or suffering. When we serve others, we serve him (see Matthew 25.37-40).

He also says that he will be present, serving others through us. Therefore, when we find people wanting to see Jesus, like the Greeks who came to Philip, we don't need to go through the same chain of command – Philip went to Andrew; Andrew went to Jesus. Jesus himself is present through us. And Jesus will be encountered in the people we meet, especially those in need.

Almighty God,
who gave such grace to your apostle Saint Andrew
that he readily obeyed the call of your Son Jesus Christ
and brought his brother with him:
call us by your holy word,
and give us grace to follow you without delay
and to tell the good news of your kingdom;
through Jesus Christ your Son our Lord,
who is alive and reigns with you,
in the unity of the Holy Spirit,
one God, now and for ever.

COLLECT

Reflection by **Stephen Cottrell**

11

Wednesday 1 December

Psalms 5, **7** or **119.1-32**
Isaiah 28.1-13
Matthew 12.38-end

Matthew 12.38-end

'... pointing to his disciples, he said, "Here are my mother and my brothers!"' (v.49)

To be the ones through whom Jesus is known today, to be his hands and heart in the midst of the world's hurt, is an awesome and privileged vocation. It is shared by everyone who is baptized into Christ.

Jesus is not callously snubbing his mother and his family in this reading. He is pointing us to realities of belonging and identity that transcend even bonds of human family.

Water is thicker than blood. This is the audacious Christian claim. We have a new belonging with each other and with God through Jesus Christ. The story of his birth that we are preparing to celebrate is the advent of the fulfilment of God's heart, and leads through cross and resurrection to a new humanity. This promise of eternal life with God and new relationship with each other is another of the great Advent themes. The sign that is even greater than the sign of Jonah is the sign of Jesus' death and resurrection, the promise of a new humanity and of life lived with God.

Judgement, in this sense, isn't about being weighed in the scales and found wanting – this is a contest no one can win and the reason Christ came in the first place! – but about being judged ready for glory.

COLLECT

Almighty God,
give us grace to cast away the works of darkness
and to put on the armour of light,
now in the time of this mortal life,
in which your Son Jesus Christ came to us in great humility;
that on the last day,
when he shall come again in his glorious majesty
    to judge the living and the dead,
we may rise to the life immortal;
through him who is alive and reigns with you,
in the unity of the Holy Spirit,
one God, now and for ever.

12 | *Reflection by* **Stephen Cottrell**

Psalms **42**, 43 *or* 14, **15**, 16
Isaiah 28.14-end
Matthew 13.1-23

Thursday 2 December

Matthew 13.1-23

'... blessed are your eyes, for they see, and your ears, for they hear'
(v.16)

Any farmer listening to the parable of the sower – and of course most of the people listening were farmers – would be outraged at the injustice of what was being said. Seed is precious. It doesn't fall on the path unless you've been stupid enough to drop it. It isn't planted in rocky ground unless you've been too lazy to have cleared and tilled the soil before you sow. Birds don't eat up. You provide a scarecrow. This feckless sower doesn't seem to know much about sowing. He doesn't deserve such an abundant harvest.

We don't hear the story this way, not just because most of us, today, are not farmers and get our food from supermarkets, but because we have the interpretation that follows, directing us to understand the story in a very particular way: it's all about the snares and temptations that we the followers of Jesus face in our discipleship. Not really about seed at all. But only the disciples get that explanation. Everyone else just had the story. A story of profligate abundance, despite failure.

'Blessed are your eyes, for they see, and your ears, for they hear', says Jesus after he has again quoted Isaiah. What we learn here is that there is more than one interpretation. We encounter both the dangers and snares of discipleship and the extravagant generosity of God. His judgement seems to be that, despite failure, blessing is given.

> Almighty God,
> as your kingdom dawns,
> turn us from the darkness of sin to the
> light of holiness,
> that we may be ready to meet you
> in our Lord and Saviour, Jesus Christ.

COLLECT

Reflection by **Stephen Cottrell**　　13

Friday 3 December

Psalms **25**, 26 *or* 17, **19**
Isaiah 29.1-14
Matthew 13.24-43

Matthew 13.24-43

'... without a parable he told them nothing' (v.34)

These words of Jesus are extremely beautiful and somewhat irritating. He teaches us in stories. Just stories. Nothing else. And as we discovered yesterday, stories can have more than one meaning. To understand the story, you have to get inside it. There is rarely a simple takeaway message, only a sit-down-and-chew-it-over invitation to dinner. What's more, Jesus tumbles one story upon another, showing us that God's kingdom can be seen and known from many different angles.

Advent is a time for us to consider what the Church calls the last things: death, judgement, heaven and hell. Eternal life.

These parables give us pictures and stories of what eternal life in God's kingdom is like. They invite us to see God's kingdom breaking in around us now – like yeast leavening the dough. Or growing among us from tiny beginnings – like mustard seeds.

Most challenging of all, Jesus tells us that the weeds and the wheat grow up alongside each other. I think we know this. We know that there is good and evil in our world. We know that the world is not divided up into angels and demons. Only frail human beings, with a great capacity for good and a terrible capacity to get it wrong.

We get ready for judgement by acknowledging this reality and asking for God's mercy, not by pretending we are just wheat.

COLLECT

Almighty God,
give us grace to cast away the works of darkness
and to put on the armour of light,
now in the time of this mortal life,
in which your Son Jesus Christ came to us in great humility;
that on the last day,
when he shall come again in his glorious majesty
    to judge the living and the dead,
we may rise to the life immortal;
through him who is alive and reigns with you,
in the unity of the Holy Spirit,
one God, now and for ever.

Reflection by **Stephen Cottrell**

Psalms **9** (10) *or* 20, 21, **23**
Isaiah 29.15-end
Matthew 13.44-end

Saturday 4 December

Matthew 13.44-end

'... they took offence at him' (v.57)

The greatest story Jesus tells is the story of his own life. He is the treasure in the field for which we would give up everything. He is the pearl of great price we seek.

Let us then move from this rich harvest of stories about God's kingdom to Jesus himself and the terrible story of how he is misunderstood, rejected, abandoned and ultimately killed by the very people he came to help.

'They took offence at him' is the terrible sentence that shouts out from this passage. Who is he to say and do these things! Just the carpenter's son.

The story of Jesus that begins in Bethlehem, a helpless baby crying out in need, ends on a cross, a crucified man crying out in pain. Those two images are the most prevalent in Christian art: Christ at his birth and Christ on the cross. They frame his life. They also frame ours. We are born, and one day we will die. We know our birthday, but each year in the calendar the day of our death, not yet known to us, passes by.

Without people's belief, Jesus isn't able to do much. After all, he's not a magician; he's God's son. But *with* belief, knowing that, in Jesus, God shares our birth and shares our death, God can do so much, leading us through death to resurrection, just as he led Jesus. This is the Advent hope.

Almighty God,
as your kingdom dawns,
turn us from the darkness of sin to the
light of holiness,
that we may be ready to meet you
in our Lord and Saviour, Jesus Christ.

COLLECT

Monday 6 December

Matthew 14.1-12

'At that time Herod the ruler heard reports about Jesus' (v.1)

We ended last week acknowledging that the greatest story Jesus told was his own life. We begin this week by seeing how the story of Jesus continues in our stories, and in all the stories of those who follow him, beginning with John the Baptist.

John was the forerunner of Jesus, the one who prepares the way. Those words – 'Prepare a way for the Lord' – echo through the Advent season. John's life and witness straddle the Old and New Testaments. He is the last of the prophets, but, in many ways, the first disciple, for John is also a follower. He famously says at Jesus' baptism that he must decrease so that Jesus can increase (John 3.30).

This is a pattern for all who follow Jesus. We follow him, and we invite others to follow. But we point to Jesus, not ourselves.

It is costly, though. John the baptizer had dared to question Herod's morality. Herod wanted to get rid of him, but was frightened of the crowds who followed John. Now that John has been put to death following a most macabre manipulation of events, Herod is frightened again. Like all weak leaders, he tries to please everyone, but ends up pleasing no one. And though he has got rid of John, Jesus is still very much alive. Thus the life of Jesus continues in all who follow him and point to him.

COLLECT

O Lord, raise up, we pray, your power
and come among us,
and with great might succour us;
that whereas, through our sins and wickedness
we are grievously hindered
in running the race that is set before us,
your bountiful grace and mercy
may speedily help and deliver us;
through Jesus Christ your Son our Lord,
to whom with you and the Holy Spirit,
be honour and glory, now and for ever.

Reflection by **Stephen Cottrell**

Psalms **56**, 57 *or* 32, **36**   **Tuesday 7 December**
Isaiah 30.19-end
Matthew 14.13-end

Matthew 14.13-end

'... he had compassion for them' (v.14)

If we think about judgement at all, we tend to be frightened of the prospect. Basil Hume, the former Roman Catholic Cardinal, once described judgement like this: he said that to be judged was to whisper the story of your life into the ear of an all-loving Father.

If judgement is about being made ready for glory, for eternal life with God, then the God who is revealed to us by Jesus as the merciful Father will have compassion on us in the same way that we see Jesus have compassion in these stories. Jesus has compassion on the crowds because they are hungry. The disciples want to send them away; Jesus wants them to stay and eat.

He takes the small offerings that are available and he feeds the crowd. He even has mastery over the storm. He pulls Peter out of the depths. His presence is a blessing; people reach out to touch the fringe of his cloak.

The compassion we see in Jesus flows from God the Father. That is why Jesus who is so compassionate to Peter and so compassionate to the crowds, also withdraws from them, so that he can be replenished by the Father's love.

We need to do the same. When we are hungry. When we are sinking. When we are in pain. Jesus' judgement is this: we are worthy; worthy of his love and welcome at his table. Worth listening to.

> Almighty God,
> purify our hearts and minds,
> that when your Son Jesus Christ comes again as
> judge and saviour
> we may be ready to receive him,
> who is our Lord and our God.

COLLECT

Reflection by **Stephen Cottrell**   17

Wednesday 8 December

Psalms **62**, 63 *or* **34**
Isaiah 31
Matthew 15.1-20

Matthew 15.1-20

'... what comes out of the mouth proceeds from the heart' (v.18)

In John's Gospel, Jesus says that the judgement is this: 'light has come into the world, and people loved darkness rather than light because their deeds were evil' (John 3.19).

The scribes and Pharisees are again trying to trap Jesus, pointing to the ways his disciples allegedly fail to follow every little point of the law. Jesus, who is always compassionate to those who acknowledge their need and know where they have gone wrong, is also quick to condemn those who judge others. Quoting Isaiah, he accuses them of only honouring God with their lips, not their lives. Making fun of their pompous hypocrisy, he entertains the crowds by ridiculing this obsession with what is eaten or not eaten. After all, says Jesus to the disciples, we all know where what we have eaten ends up: down the sewer!

No, says Jesus, it is not what goes into your mouth, but what comes out that truly matters. Therefore, as Jesus says in Luke's Gospel: 'Be merciful, just as your Father is merciful' (Luke 6.36).

We, too, must pay attention to what comes out of our mouths, praying that our words and actions may be merciful and compassionate. Just as Jesus is quick to condemn those who are quick to condemn, he is quick to forgive those who seek forgiveness and who are ready to forgive others.

COLLECT

O Lord, raise up, we pray, your power
and come among us,
and with great might succour us;
that whereas, through our sins and wickedness
we are grievously hindered
in running the race that is set before us,
your bountiful grace and mercy
may speedily help and deliver us;
through Jesus Christ your Son our Lord,
to whom with you and the Holy Spirit,
be honour and glory, now and for ever.

18 | *Reflection by* **Stephen Cottrell**

Psalms 53, **54**, 60 *or* **37***
Isaiah 32
Matthew 15.21-28

Thursday 9 December

Matthew 15.21-28

'Woman, great is your faith!' (v.28)

Now here is an interesting story because, it seems, Jesus is the one being judged ... The Canaanite woman asks Jesus for mercy, but he ignores her. The disciples urge him to send her away because she is badgering them as well. Jesus doesn't show compassion; he just rather rudely reminds everyone present that he has come for the 'lost sheep of the house of Israel' (and therefore not for foreigners like her). But she persists. She kneels before Jesus and pleads for help.

Jesus appears unmoved. 'It isn't fair to take the children's food and throw it to the dogs,' he replies. Her answer is brilliant. 'Yes, Lord, yet even the dogs eat the crumbs that fall from their masters' table.' It turns Jesus around. He is astounded by her faithfulness. Her daughter is healed. What's going on here?

Might it be this? Jesus himself is learning and refining his vocation to be the one through whom God's merciful judgement is going to be made available to everyone, not just Israel. For Jesus, this journey of fully understanding his vocation to be the light of the world reaches its climax in Gethsemane and Calvary. This woman helps him get there.

Vocation is learned, not just received. Judgement is also a journey of becoming. On the way we all need challenge – as it turns out, even Jesus. So, therefore, we definitely do too!

Almighty God,
purify our hearts and minds,
that when your Son Jesus Christ comes again as
judge and saviour
we may be ready to receive him,
who is our Lord and our God.

COLLECT

Reflection by **Stephen Cottrell**   19

Friday 10 December

Matthew 15.29-end

'... they praised the God of Israel' (v.31)

In Luke's Gospel, the followers of John the Baptist come to Jesus asking whether he is the one promised from God, or whether they should wait for another. Jesus answers by pointing to the things he does: 'the blind receive their sight, the lame walk, the lepers are cleansed, the deaf hear, the dead are raised, the poor have good news brought to them' (Luke 7.22).

In today's reading, the crowds come to Jesus again. They bring with them 'the lame, the maimed, the blind, the mute, and many others'. They put them at Jesus' feet, and he cures them.

In Jesus, God's promises and God's future break into our present. If Advent is about getting ready to see God clearly and to enjoy eternal life with God, then these are the signs of what the reign of God will be like: tears wiped away and the sick healed.

It is hard for us to imagine this. Our world is besieged by sickness, poverty and injustice. Yet still we need to bring ourselves and bring others to Jesus. Then we will be able to see God clearly and see clearly where our world needs to change.

God's Church will be most like Jesus when we turn outwards to feed and heal and teach, and when we remember the poor. It is our willingness to do this – or otherwise – that will be the criterion of judgement. Then people will praise God.

COLLECT

O Lord, raise up, we pray, your power
and come among us,
and with great might succour us;
that whereas, through our sins and wickedness
we are grievously hindered
in running the race that is set before us,
your bountiful grace and mercy
may speedily help and deliver us;
through Jesus Christ your Son our Lord,
to whom with you and the Holy Spirit,
be honour and glory, now and for ever.

Reflection by **Stephen Cottrell**

Psalm **145** *or* 41, **42**, 43
Isaiah 35
Matthew 16.1-12

Saturday 11 December

Matthew 16.1-12

'Then he left them and went away.' (v.4)

We end this week with these hard words: Jesus left them and went away.

The Pharisees and Sadducees want signs. As if what Jesus has said and done is not already enough! The disciples are covered in confusion and muddle. Isn't that always the case? Now, as well as then.

The only sign that is given is the sign of Jonah. But what is the sign of Jonah? Is it the sign of redemption: Jonah spewed out of the whale after three days, an anticipation of Jesus' resurrection? Or is it the message of Jonah to Nineveh: repent or die?

Or is it that we need to work out our own discipleship? That God has given us freedom and responsibility to carry forward the mission of Jesus in the world today? Is it like Jesus saying to Mary Magdalene, do not cling to me?

Like the first disciples, maybe the main problem is that we forget to bring bread; forget to depend on the living bread of God's word, the sacramental bread of God's presence?

As the thoughts of Advent that look to the last things, turn towards Christmas, and God's first things, let us receive the vocation to be God's presence in the world, shining as brightly as the star over Bethlehem, sustained by the bread of God's continuing presence with us. Until that day when we see him face to face.

Almighty God,
purify our hearts and minds,
that when your Son Jesus Christ comes again as
judge and saviour
we may be ready to receive him,
who is our Lord and our God.

COLLECT

Reflection by **Stephen Cottrell**   21

Monday 13 December

Matthew 16.13-end

'But who do you say that I am?' (v.15)

Today we encounter Peter, both at his brightest and his dimmest – he catches a glimpse of the reality that yes, this man Jesus is the long-awaited Messiah, yet fails to recognize the truth about the nature of Christ's identity. He gets it badly wrong and is reprimanded severely.

The gap between Peter's rise and fall, as it were, is his lack of understanding about the place of suffering in the journey of faith. He had visions of a powerful political Messiah come to overthrow the oppressive Roman rule but instead was confronted by talk of taking up his cross and losing his life. Over 2000 years later, I wonder if we too are still sometimes caught in the horns of exactly the same dilemma, acknowledging Jesus as Lord but not fully grasping the significance of that for our lives and for the Church.

This passage makes crystal clear the implications of following Christ and lays bare the cost of discipleship. As church communities and as individuals seeking to understand who Jesus is for us, we do well to remember we have not been promised prosperity and success, power and position. Rather we are called to witness faithfully to a saviour whose obedience took him even to death on a cross. We are to offer ourselves in humble service of others confident that, though we may lose everything, in Christ we are made whole.

COLLECT

O Lord Jesus Christ,
who at your first coming sent your messenger
to prepare your way before you:
grant that the ministers and stewards of your mysteries
may likewise so prepare and make ready your way
by turning the hearts of the disobedient to the wisdom of the just,
that at your second coming to judge the world
we may be found an acceptable people in your sight;
for you are alive and reign with the Father
in the unity of the Holy Spirit,
one God, now and for ever.

Reflection by **Guli Francis-Dehqani**

Tuesday 14 December

Matthew 17.1-13

'This is my Son, the Beloved' (v.5)

Do you recognize that feeling of being in an unexpected situation, not of your own making, unsure what to do or say, and eventually covering your awkwardness with a rush of words or activity?

I wonder whether Peter, James and John felt something of that as they witnessed Jesus' transfiguration and the appearance of Moses and Elijah. In this highly charged and emotional scene, it's hardly surprising they were utterly bewildered and, to fill the silence and make themselves feel useful, they started talking about building shelters. God then literally interrupted their busyness with an echo from Jesus' baptism in Matthew 3, 'This is my Son, the Beloved, with him I am well pleased'. Words of love and affirmation, and a reminder that the most important thing about Jesus' ministry was not all the activity but the relationship with his father. Everything he said and did emanated from his identity as the Beloved of God.

As God in human form, Jesus invites us to recognize something of this patterning in our own lives too. It is perhaps the greatest gift and yet the hardest to receive – to know that you are a beloved child of God, to feel at the core of your being that this is what gives you value, over and above your greatest successes and achievements. It can take a lifetime to fully understand this truth, but once grasped, its power is transformative.

God for whom we watch and wait,
you sent John the Baptist to prepare the way of your Son:
give us courage to speak the truth,
to hunger for justice,
and to suffer for the cause of right,
with Jesus Christ our Lord.

COLLECT

Reflection by **Guli Francis-Dehqani** | 23

Wednesday 15 December

Psalms **75**, 96 *or* **119.57-80**
Isaiah 39
Matthew 17.14-21

Matthew 17.14-21

'... the disciples came to Jesus' (v.19)

This is one of those difficult incidents that at first sight can be confusing and disheartening. It's worth remembering that the verses follow immediately on from the account of Jesus' transfiguration. As such we can't help but notice two striking contrasts that need to be held in tension. The glory of God's presence evident in the transfiguration does not remove the reality of suffering in the world (exemplified here by the boy with epilepsy), nor does experiencing that glory (as the disciples did) guarantee success even in matters of faith. Put another way, pain and anguish will always be with us, as will our failures and weaknesses but neither can undermine the splendour, mercy or compassion of God.

If that's our starting place, what positive message can we take from this passage? Here are three brief thoughts to reflect on. First, despite their failure and the disappointment that must have stung badly, the disciples *stay with Jesus*. They remain alongside him, eager to learn and deepen their faith – sometimes that's all we can manage, and that's OK. Second, together with the disciples, perhaps we come to see that faith is not so much about specific beliefs or intellectual understanding but about *trust* in a growing relationship. And finally, faith – even in small amounts – enables and empowers, whereas its lack weakens and diminishes.

COLLECT

O Lord Jesus Christ,
who at your first coming sent your messenger
to prepare your way before you:
grant that the ministers and stewards of your mysteries
may likewise so prepare and make ready your way
by turning the hearts of the disobedient to the wisdom of the just,
that at your second coming to judge the world
we may be found an acceptable people in your sight;
for you are alive and reign with the Father
in the unity of the Holy Spirit,
one God, now and for ever.

Reflection by **Guli Francis-Dehqani**

Thursday 16 December

Matthew 17.22-end

'... so that we do not give offence' (v.27)

Fearless and outspoken as Jesus is on occasions, he can also be the master of diplomacy, avoiding traps or refusing to cause unnecessary offence. This curious episode is one such occasion providing an abject lesson to those of us eager to ensure that our way wins or that our point is loudly made.

The temple tax mentioned in verse 24 probably refers to a tax imposed either for the upkeep of the temple or specifically to maintain the sacrificial system in Jerusalem. Either way, Jesus is against the tax, arguing that just like a king would never tax his own family, so God would not tax his people Israel. However, Jesus also recognizes that for some, the tax is considered a religious duty and so he pays it, notably not from his own pocket, but using a lost coin found in a fish.

How wedded are you to particular forms of worship and spirituality? What is your response and how do you act when you are in a church different from your own, with traditions and conventions you don't understand and maybe even disagree with? It's so easy to take the moral high ground, refuse to participate or look down on the practices of others. Jesus reminds us that our actions, even those we hold dear, should always take into account the feelings of others. Sometimes we are on holy ground and we do well to tread carefully and gently.

God for whom we watch and wait,
you sent John the Baptist to prepare the way of your Son:
give us courage to speak the truth,
to hunger for justice,
and to suffer for the cause of right,
with Jesus Christ our Lord.

COLLECT

Friday 17 December

Psalms 77, **98** or **51**, 54
Zephaniah 3.1-13
Matthew 18.1-20

Matthew 18.1-20

'... these little ones' (v.6)

A large portion of today's passage reads rather like a manifesto for children and young people. It puts them centre stage, giving them their rightful place as cherished human beings within the community of believers – and this at a time when children had little value and few rights. Jesus' sentiments are entirely counter-cultural and he uses some of his harshest words for those who would harm or hurt children, and it is spine-chilling.

In these weeks leading up to Christmas, children are often more in our minds than usual: the stars of all those nativity plays, the purest expression of Christmas joy, the sounds of singing and laughter. But we do well to remember that our responsibility towards the welfare of children is an all-year requirement. The Church has often fallen gravely short in this area, but, in truth, the safety and protection of children should be at the heart of all we do. This is not just a moral imperative but a theological one, central to our faith and how we build communities.

If this is true for children, it is also true of other vulnerable people – those undermined and undervalued by society. Ultimately, the Church will be judged by how we treat those who are weakest and most powerless, and lest we forget, the baby whom we wait to greet on Christmas morning is our ever present reminder.

COLLECT

O Lord Jesus Christ,
who at your first coming sent your messenger
to prepare your way before you:
grant that the ministers and stewards of your mysteries
may likewise so prepare and make ready your way
by turning the hearts of the disobedient to the wisdom of the just,
that at your second coming to judge the world
we may be found an acceptable people in your sight;
for you are alive and reign with the Father
in the unity of the Holy Spirit,
one God, now and for ever.

*Reflection by **Guli Francis-Dehqani***

Psalm **71** *or* **68**
Zephaniah 3.14-end
Matthew 18.21-end

Saturday 18 December

Matthew 18.21-end

*'... out of pity for him, the lord of that slave released him
and forgave him' (v.27)*

You could argue that the thorny topic of forgiveness hasn't always
been served well in the Church. It can all too easily be used flippantly,
leading to the accusation that Christians don't take justice seriously,
or it can be imposed on those who have suffered harm and abuse,
making them feel guilty if they are unable to forgive. Forgiveness, far
from being a simple equation, is a messy process and immensely
complex. It should be handled with great care and with concern for
the safety and welfare of the most vulnerable.

That said, forgiveness remains a central Christian tenet and one we
can't circumvent. That we must each recognize our own need of
forgiveness and in turn extend it to those who cause us hurt is at the
heart of our faith, and we are called to practise it in smaller and
larger ways. This is far from easy, but the rewards are precious:
forgiveness offers redemption to the offender and freedom from
anger and bitterness for the one wronged.

The *desire to forgive* is often the starting place for what can be a
long journey with twists and turns. The story in today's Bible passage
helps us understand that in order to forgive, first we need
compassion – the ability to put ourselves in another's shoes and see
the world from their perspective. With compassion in our hearts and
with God's grace, we can find the way towards, 'father forgive'.

God for whom we watch and wait,
you sent John the Baptist to prepare the way of your Son:
give us courage to speak the truth,
to hunger for justice,
and to suffer for the cause of right,
with Jesus Christ our Lord.

COLLECT

Reflection by **Guli Francis-Dehqani** | 27

Monday 20 December

Psalms **46**, 95
Malachi 1.1, 6-end
Matthew 19.1-12

Matthew 19.1-12

'Let anyone accept this who can' (v.12)

Today, we encounter Jesus once more in the company of the Pharisees who are wanting to catch him out over a controversial issue of the day. In Jewish law, divorce was permitted, but arguments continued over whether or not it was only permissible on some legitimate grounds.

Jesus responds by doing two things. First, and typically for him, he reframes the debate from the negative (grounds for divorce) to the positive (grounds for marriage): God made them male and female so they may become one flesh. Second, he distinguishes between the perfect will of God and the Commandments, which allowed for human sin. He thereby shifts from what may be legally possible towards a radical demand for conformity to God's will as expressed in the beginning. Arguably, however, this purity of heart that Jesus envisions is an impossible ideal for mere mortals and hence our need of God's grace and forgiveness in all our shortcomings and failings.

Still, it's possible to see from these verses why the question of divorce and remarriage remains difficult for some Christians today. But most have concluded that, in some cases, it is not only permissible but maybe even preferable – the lesser of two evils. And lest we be tempted to judge, perhaps we should call to mind those other words of Jesus uttered when the woman was caught in adultery: let the one without sin cast the first stone.

COLLECT

God our redeemer,
who prepared the Blessed Virgin Mary
to be the mother of your Son:
grant that, as she looked for his coming as our saviour,
so we may be ready to greet him
when he comes again as our judge;
who is alive and reigns with you,
in the unity of the Holy Spirit,
one God, now and for ever.

| *Reflection by* **Guli Francis-Dehqani**

Psalms **121**, 122, 123
Malachi 2.1-16
Matthew 19.13-15

Tuesday 21 December

Matthew 19.13-15

'Let the little children come to me' (v.14)

Like most parents, I'd easily say my children always come first. As they've grown older and my working life has become busier, I still remind them that when push comes to shove, I'd gladly drop everything to be there if they need me. And I mean it … except that sometimes I fall short.

Over the years there have been occasions when one or other of them has been ill on a particularly inconvenient day. I've begrudgingly cancelled appointments or made my excuses for meetings I should have attended, feeling guilty about not fulfilling my responsibilities or letting people down.

But without fail, on each occasion, I've come to realize soon enough that I made the right decision. Not just because I did what a mother should do, but because the unexpected time has been a precious gift and a reminder of all the blessings my children have given me and the way in which they continue to enrich my life.

This Christmas season, who are the treasured people in your life that you need to make time for – those whom you might sometimes think of as an inconvenience, just as the disciples did with the little ones who came to Jesus? Who are those who can all too easily get squeezed out of your life by the pressure of all your other responsibilities? Who knows what blessings await you if you make time just to be with them.

Eternal God,
as Mary waited for the birth of your Son,
so we wait for his coming in glory;
bring us through the birth pangs of this present age
to see, with her, our great salvation
in Jesus Christ our Lord.

COLLECT

Reflection by **Guli Francis-Dehqani**

Wednesday 22 December

Psalms **124**, 125, 126, 127
Malachi 2.17 – 3.12
Matthew 19.16-end

Matthew 19.16-end

'... you will have treasure in heaven' (v.21)

With my family I left our homeland of Iran suddenly and unexpectedly after traumatic events around the 1979 Islamic Revolution. We left behind all we owned, each bringing just one suitcase hurriedly packed. My parents lost their home and everything they possessed. Soon, however, they began rebuilding their lives and I noticed how they still took pleasure in the material things that filled their home. But what I noticed too was their disposition towards these belongings. Though they still valued and enjoyed them, there was a lightness in the attachment. They were generous to a fault and lived as those who knew what the really important things in life are. Had they lost everything a second time, they would still have remained the joyful, faith-filled people they always were.

Today's passage is more about priorities than about how rich or poor we are per se. The young man was challenged by Jesus to sell all his possessions not so much because he was too rich but because he had grown too attached to his belongings. They were damaging his relationship with God and his capacity to be generous. Jesus' words are a reminder of how easy it is to lose sight of our priorities.

In the busyness of preparing for Christmas, it might be helpful to take a moment to consider what things get in the way of our relationships, both with God and with others.

COLLECT

God our redeemer,
who prepared the Blessed Virgin Mary
to be the mother of your Son:
grant that, as she looked for his coming as our saviour,
so we may be ready to greet him
when he comes again as our judge;
who is alive and reigns with you,
in the unity of the Holy Spirit,
one God, now and for ever.

| *Reflection by* **Guli Francis-Dehqani**

Psalms 128, 129, **130**, 131
Malachi 3.13 – end of 4
Matthew 23.1-12

Thursday 23 December

Matthew 23.1-12

'They tie up heavy burdens ... and lay them on the shoulders of others' (v.4)

The American author and Unitarian Minister Robert Fulghum is reputed to have said, 'Don't worry that children never listen to you; worry that they're always watching you'. Wise words, and an object lesson for parents and all who have dealings with children and young people. Similarly, Jesus tells his disciples to do as the scribes and Pharisees teach but not as they do, for they are hypocrites and there is disparity between their words and actions.

I recall hearing my father preach a sermon in the early days of the revolution in Iran as the Christian community was facing the very real possibility of suffering and persecution. It was early 1979 and I was 12 years old, but it's remained with me ever since. 'I have been speaking about forgiveness for many years', he said, 'but now the time is coming when I will have to learn to live it.'

The disparity between words and actions is a perennial problem for the Church generally. Over the centuries, Jesus' words of love and welcome, of compassion, generosity and reconciliation have been preached far and wide. And yet so often as Christian communities we struggle to embody the radical inclusion that the message demands. Practising what we preach can be demanding and sometimes costly, but it's worth reminding ourselves that ultimately we will be remembered for how we behaved and we will be judged more by our actions than our words.

Eternal God,
as Mary waited for the birth of your Son,
so we wait for his coming in glory;
bring us through the birth pangs of this present age
to see, with her, our great salvation
in Jesus Christ our Lord.

COLLECT

Reflection by **Guli Francis-Dehqani** | 31

Friday 24 December
Christmas Eve

Matthew 23.13-28

'... the altar that makes the gift sacred' (v.19)

It might at first seem like we can relax a little on reading today's passage, despite its harsh tone and recurring chorus of 'woe to you'. After all, it's not you and me being addressed, but the scribes and Pharisees. We, on the other hand, are seeking to live the life of faith honestly and devotedly. Well, I invite you to look deep into your heart and reflect more searchingly.

The entire extract sounds for me like a warning bell, a reminder of how easy it is to get religion wrong. The scribes and Pharisees were probably trying their best, following the law and teaching the tenets of faith. But repeatedly they got it wrong. For us too, I wonder if it's all too easy to live as those constrained by the rules, bound by the doctrines, trying to do the right thing but missing the real point, the weightier matters of justice, mercy and faith. How much time and energy do we spend, even as Christians, disagreeing with one another over details of the law instead of building relationships across our differences, seeking the face of Christ in each other.

This Christmas Eve, let's pause for a moment and pray for the Church. Let's remember the gift we are offered in the Christ child who did not come for us to argue and fall out over but as the gracious and loving cause of our worship and wonder.

COLLECT

Almighty God,
you make us glad with the yearly remembrance
    of the birth of your Son Jesus Christ:
grant that, as we joyfully receive him as our redeemer,
so we may with sure confidence behold him
when he shall come to be our judge;
who is alive and reigns with you,
in the unity of the Holy Spirit,
one God, now and for ever.

| *Reflection by* **Guli Francis-Dehqani**

Continue your seasonal journey with

At the heart of Christmas
12 Days of stories and meditations for Christmas

by **Archbishops Justin Welby,
Stephen Cottrell** and guests

Available now from
www.chpublishing.co.uk

Morning Prayer – a simple form

Preparation

O Lord, open our lips
and our mouth shall proclaim your praise.

A prayer of thanksgiving for Advent

Blessed are you, Sovereign God of all,
to you be praise and glory for ever.
In your tender compassion
the dawn from on high is breaking upon us
to dispel the lingering shadows of night.
As we look for your coming among us this day,
open our eyes to behold your presence
and strengthen our hands to do your will,
that the world may rejoice and give you praise.
Blessed be God, Father, Son and Holy Spirit.
Blessed be God for ever.

Word of God

Psalmody *(the psalm or psalms listed for the day)*

**Glory to the Father and to the Son
and to the Holy Spirit;
as it was in the beginning is now:
and shall be for ever. Amen.**

Reading from Holy Scripture *(one or both of the passages set for the day)*

Reflection

The Benedictus (The Song of Zechariah) *(see opposite page)*

Prayers

Intercessions – a time of prayer for the day and its tasks, the world and its need, the church and her life.

The Collect for the Day

The Lord's Prayer *(see p. 37)*

Conclusion

A blessing or the Grace *(see p. 37)*, or a concluding response

Let us bless the Lord
Thanks be to God

Benedictus (The Song of Zechariah)

1 Blessed be the Lord the God of Israel, ♦
 who has come to his people and set them free.

2 He has raised up for us a mighty Saviour, ♦
 born of the house of his servant David.

3 Through his holy prophets God promised of old ♦
 to save us from our enemies,
  from the hands of all that hate us,

4 To show mercy to our ancestors, ♦
 and to remember his holy covenant.

5 This was the oath God swore to our father Abraham: ♦
 to set us free from the hands of our enemies,

6 Free to worship him without fear, ♦
 holy and righteous in his sight
  all the days of our life.

7 And you, child, shall be called the prophet of the Most High, ♦
 for you will go before the Lord to prepare his way,

8 To give his people knowledge of salvation ♦
 by the forgiveness of all their sins.

9 In the tender compassion of our God ♦
 the dawn from on high shall break upon us,

10 To shine on those who dwell in darkness
  and the shadow of death, ♦
 and to guide our feet into the way of peace.

Luke 1.68-79

**Glory to the Father and to the Son
and to the Holy Spirit;
as it was in the beginning is now:
and shall be for ever. Amen.**

Seasonal Prayers of Thanksgiving

Advent

Blessed are you, Sovereign God of all,
to you be praise and glory for ever.
In your tender compassion
the dawn from on high is breaking upon us
to dispel the lingering shadows of night.
As we look for your coming among us this day,
open our eyes to behold your presence
and strengthen our hands to do your will,
that the world may rejoice and give you praise.
Blessed be God, Father, Son and Holy Spirit.
Blessed be God for ever.

At Any Time

Blessed are you, creator of all,
to you be praise and glory for ever.
As your dawn renews the face of the earth
bringing light and life to all creation,
may we rejoice in this day you have made;
as we wake refreshed from the depths of sleep,
open our eyes to behold your presence
and strengthen our hands to do your will,
that the world may rejoice and give you praise.
Blessed be God, Father, Son and Holy Spirit.
Blessed be God for ever.

after Lancelot Andrewes (1626)

The Lord's Prayer and The Grace

Our Father in heaven,
hallowed be your name,
your kingdom come,
your will be done,
on earth as in heaven.
Give us today our daily bread.
Forgive us our sins
as we forgive those who sin against us.
Lead us not into temptation
but deliver us from evil.
For the kingdom, the power,
and the glory are yours
now and for ever.
Amen.

(or)

Our Father, who art in heaven,
hallowed be thy name;
thy kingdom come;
thy will be done;
on earth as it is in heaven.
Give us this day our daily bread.
And forgive us our trespasses,
as we forgive those who trespass against us.
And lead us not into temptation;
but deliver us from evil.
For thine is the kingdom,
the power and the glory,
for ever and ever.
Amen.

The grace of our Lord Jesus Christ,
and the love of God,
and the fellowship of the Holy Spirit,
be with us all evermore.
Amen.

An Order for Night Prayer (Compline)

The Lord almighty grant us a quiet night and a perfect end.
Amen.

Our help is in the name of the Lord
who made heaven and earth.

A period of silence for reflection on the past day may follow.

The following or other suitable words of penitence may be used

Most merciful God,
we confess to you,
before the whole company of heaven and one another,
that we have sinned in thought, word and deed
and in what we have failed to do.
Forgive us our sins,
heal us by your Spirit
and raise us to new life in Christ. Amen.

O God, make speed to save us.
O Lord, make haste to help us.

Glory to the Father and to the Son
and to the Holy Spirit;
as it was in the beginning is now
and shall be for ever. Amen.
Alleluia.

The following or another suitable hymn may be sung

Before the ending of the day,
Creator of the world, we pray
That you, with steadfast love, would keep
Your watch around us while we sleep.

From evil dreams defend our sight,
From fears and terrors of the night;
Tread underfoot our deadly foe
That we no sinful thought may know.

O Father, that we ask be done
Through Jesus Christ, your only Son;
And Holy Spirit, by whose breath
Our souls are raised to life from death.

The Word of God

Psalmody

One or more of Psalms 4, 91 or 134 may be used.

Psalm 134

1   Come, bless the Lord, all you servants of the Lord, ♦
    you that by night stand in the house of the Lord.

2   Lift up your hands towards the sanctuary ♦
    and bless the Lord.

3   The Lord who made heaven and earth ♦
    give you blessing out of Zion.

Glory to the Father and to the Son
and to the Holy Spirit;
as it was in the beginning is now
and shall be for ever. Amen.

Scripture Reading

One of the following short lessons or another suitable
passage is read

You, O Lord, are in the midst of us and we are called by your
name; leave us not, O Lord our God.

Jeremiah 14.9

(or)

Be sober, be vigilant, because your adversary the devil is
prowling round like a roaring lion, seeking for someone
to devour. Resist him, strong in the faith.

I Peter 5.8,9

(or)

The servants of the Lamb shall see the face of God, whose name
will be on their foreheads. There will be no more night: they will
not need the light of a lamp or the light of the sun, for God will
be their light, and they will reign for ever and ever.

Revelation 22.4,5

Into your hands, O Lord, I commend my spirit.
Into your hands, O Lord, I commend my spirit.
For you have redeemed me, Lord God of truth.
I commend my spirit.
Glory to the Father and to the Son
and to the Holy Spirit.
Into your hands, O Lord, I commend my spirit.

Or, in Easter

Into your hands, O Lord, I commend my spirit.
Alleluia, alleluia.
Into your hands, O Lord, I commend my spirit.
Alleluia, alleluia.
For you have redeemed me, Lord God of truth.
Alleluia, alleluia.
Glory to the Father and to the Son
and to the Holy Spirit.
Into your hands, O Lord, I commend my spirit.
Alleluia, alleluia.

Keep me as the apple of your eye.
Hide me under the shadow of your wings.

Gospel Canticle

Nunc Dimittis (The Song of Simeon)

Save us, O Lord, while waking,
and guard us while sleeping,
that awake we may watch with Christ
and asleep may rest in peace.

1   Now, Lord, you let your servant go in peace:
      your word has been fulfilled.

2   My own eyes have seen the salvation
      which you have prepared in the sight of every people;

3   A light to reveal you to the nations
      and the glory of your people Israel.

Luke 2.29-32

**Glory to the Father and to the Son
and to the Holy Spirit;
as it was in the beginning is now
and shall be for ever. Amen.**

**Save us, O Lord, while waking,
and guard us while sleeping,
that awake we may watch with Christ
and asleep may rest in peace.**

Prayers

Intercessions and thanksgivings may be offered here.

The Collect

Visit this place, O Lord, we pray,
and drive far from it the snares of the enemy;
may your holy angels dwell with us and guard us in peace,
and may your blessing be always upon us;
through Jesus Christ our Lord.
Amen.

The Lord's Prayer (see p. 37) may be said.

The Conclusion

In peace we will lie down and sleep;
for you alone, Lord, make us dwell in safety.

Abide with us, Lord Jesus,
for the night is at hand and the day is now past.

As the night watch looks for the morning,
so do we look for you, O Christ.

[Come with the dawning of the day
and make yourself known in the breaking of the bread.]

The Lord bless us and watch over us;
the Lord make his face shine upon us and be gracious to us;
the Lord look kindly on us and give us peace.
Amen.

Love what you've read?

Why not consider using *Reflections for Daily Prayer* all year round? We also publish these Bible reflections in an annual format, containing material for the entire Church year.

The volume for the **2021/22** Church year is now available and features contributions from a host of distinguished writers: Justine Allain Chapman, Joanna Collicutt, Stephen Cottrell, Azariah France-Williams, Guli Francis-Dehqani, Malcolm Guite, Isabelle Hamley, Colin Heber-Percy, Christopher Herbert, David Hoyle, John Inge, Rachel Mann, Anna Matthews, Peter Moger, Philip North, Karen O'Donnell, Brother Sam SSF, Angela Tilby, Rachel Treweek, Catherine Williams and Rowan Williams.

REFLECTIONS FOR DAILY PRAYER
Advent 2021 to the eve of Advent 2022

ISBN 978 0 7151 2383 6   **£16.99** • 336 pages

Please note: this book reproduces the material for Advent found in the volume you are now holding.

Reflections for Daily Prayer 2022/23 will be available from May 2022 with reflections written by: Kate Bruce, Vanessa Conant, Steven Croft, Paula Gooder, Helen-Ann Hartley, Jonathan Frost, Luigi Gioia, Michael Ipgrave, Mark Ireland, Graham James, Libby Lane, Jan McFarlane, Mark Oakley, John Perumbalath, Sharon Prentis, John Pritchard, Sarah Rowland Jones and Jane Williams.

REFLECTIONS FOR DAILY PRAYER
Advent 2022 to the eve of Advent 2023

ISBN 978 0 7151 2396 6   **£16.99** • 336 pages

REFLECTIONS FOR SUNDAYS (YEAR C)

Reflections for Sundays offers over 250 reflections on the Principal Readings for every Sunday and major Holy Day in Year C, from the same experienced team of writers that have made *Reflections for Daily Prayer* so successful. For each Sunday and major Holy Day, they provide:

- full lectionary details for the Principal Service
- a reflection on each Old Testament reading (both Continuous and Related)
- a reflection on the Epistle
- a reflection on the Gospel.

This book also contains a substantial introduction to the Gospel of Luke, written by Paula Gooder.

£14.99 • 288 pages
ISBN 978 1 78140 039 5

Also available in Kindle and epub formats

REFLECTIONS FOR LENT 2022

Wednesday 2 March – Saturday 16 April 2022

This shortened edition of *Reflections* is ideal for group or church use during Lent, or for anyone seeking a daily devotional guide to this most holy season of the Christian year. It is also an ideal taster for those wanting to begin a regular pattern of prayer and reading.

Authors: Christopher Herbert, Philip North, Angela Tilby, Rachel Treweek, *with Holy Week reflections by* Rowan Williams

£4.99 • 64 pages
ISBN 978 1 78140 276 4
Available November 2021

REFLECTIONS FOR DAILY PRAYER
App

Make Bible study and reflection a part of your routine wherever you go with the Reflections for Daily Prayer App for Apple and Android devices.

Download the app for free from the App Store (Apple devices) or Google Play (Android devices) and receive a week's worth of reflections free. Then purchase a monthly, three-monthly or annual subscription to receive up-to-date content.